Table of Contents

1 INTRODUCTION

This is a hypothesis. A hypothesis is an assumption; a guess. A tentative statement to be proven or disproved by evidence. It is a tentative explanation of observed facts. It is an unproved theory tentatively accepted to explain certain facts, supposition or assumption. In science, a hypothesis is an idea concerning an event and its possible explanation. The term is one favored by the followers of the philosopher Karl Popper who argue that the merit of a scientific hypothesis lies in its ability to make testable predictions. A hypothesis is assumed to be tenable for the purposes of investigation. A hypothesis can be confirmed by experiments which are observations under controlled conditions. When observations or experimental data do not support the hypothesis, it must be changed or discarded. Every theory or law in science begins as a hypothesis.

This paper is about the disease autism. Autism is not a mental disease. Children with autism are not unruly kids with behavioral problems. Autism is not caused by bad parents who gave their children too little attention. Most importantly, no known factors in the psychological environment of a child have been shown to cause autism.

Autism is a developmental disability that typically appears during the first three years of life. Autism is the result of a neurological disorder that affects the functioning of the brain. Autism and its associated behaviors occur in approximately 15 of every 10,000 individuals. Autism is four times more prevalent in boys than girls and knows no racial, ethnic, or social boundaries. Family income, lifestyle, or educational levels do not affect the chances of occurrence.

The mechanism of this condition is probably due to an inherent constitutional defect. Some have implicated emotional factors because mothers of these children have been described as distant and emotionally cool. These maternal attitudes on the other hand may well be the mother's reaction to the unloving child, for love must be reciprocated to endure. Several old theories about the cause of autism have been proven false.

2 AUTISM THE DIAGNOSIS

Early infantile autism was first described by Kanner in 1943. According to Kanner the symptoms of infantile autism appear early in life or are present from the beginning. He and others maintain that early infantile autism is different from childhood schizophrenia. The autistic children do not withdraw from formerly existing participation with others as in the case of schizophrenia, but rather they display an extreme autistic aloneness from the start.

The pathognomonic disorder was seen as the children's inability to relate themselves in the ordinary way to people and situations from the beginning of life. The second distinctive feature noted by Kanner was failure to use language for the purpose of communication. Thus, Kanner had delineated a syndrome that is differentiated from childhood schizophrenia by virtue of detachment starting no later than the first year of life and from oligophrenia by evidence of good intellectual potential.

These children have many other problems. An early sign of autism is indifference to those who give care; an infant may not respond to affection or being picked up. They are not responsive to their mothers. They resist cuddling and do not display the usual anticipatory responses and postures for being picked up and cradled. The child does not respond to external stimuli or adapt himself to the other individual.

An autistic infant is unable to make contact with his environment. They seem isolated from their environment and are more likely to relate to objects than people. There is resultant aloofness.

Autism is a condition characterized by a preoccupation with fantasy and lack of concern for reality. Autism generally implies that the material of their thinking derives from the subject himself, appearing in the nature of daydreams, fantasies, delusions, and hallucinations, which substitute for reality in wish fulfillment.

Symptoms appear early in life or are present from the beginning: self absorption, inaccessibility, aloneness, inability to relate, highly repetitive play, and rage reactions if interrupted; predilection for rhythmical movements such as rolling, jumping, rocking, and whirling, and many language disturbances such as echolalia. This sort of thinking can be found in children now known as autistic and those who are diagnosed as child schizophrenics. Ambivalence is expressed in uncertain hesitant affect.

There is a disease so similar to infant autism that it has confused psychiatrists for years. Eugene Bleuler [1911] believed the essential disease to be the splitting of the personality shown in four main ways: disturbances of associations, disturbances of affect, autism, and heightened ambivalence often called the "four A's. When associations link between thoughts are loosened or destroyed, looseness of associations occur and bizarre, illogical, and chaotic thinking results. When affect is split it becomes inappropriate and mood is exaggerated, indifferent, shallow, or flattened. The combined result of these four disturbances is that the patient is unable to organize meaningful, logical, consistent thoughts, behavior, or interactions.

There are other children who can easily become diagnosed as autistic but suffer from other problems. Psychosis may be found in children who are brain damaged or mentally retarded. Differentiation between mental retardation and schizophrenia of childhood is often difficult, and many psychotic children have been called retarded because of their inaccessibility.

The term, 'Infantile autism' has become increasingly fashionable as a diagnosis but with concomitant dilution of its specificity. Confusion with other children's psychiatric problems has been a difficulty for therapists from the start. One of the reasons for this is the name of the disease. Autism is both a disease and a human mental mechanism. Autism refers to a subjective, self-centered, type of thinking manifested by a tendency to apply personal and private meanings to situations, and to words, rather than con-sensually validated ones. It is a form of thinking more or less genuinely of a subjective character; if objective material enters it is given subjective meaning and emphasis.

3 ORGANIC ABNORMALITIES

Although Johns Hopkins studies were negative with respect to organic abnormalities, other investigators have drawn different conclusions. Grant stated that neurological disorders underlie the majority of cases of autism and schizophrenia in childhood. Shain and Yannet have demonstrated 50 cases of autism from the Southbury Training School. They reported a high percentage of seizures, EEG abnormalities and associated neurological findings. These studies together with a number of reports on small groups of autistic children with gross EEG or neurological disorders, are open to serious questions as to diagnostic specificity.

Some autistic children have enlarged ventricles [hollow areas] in the brain. Signs of damage show up on X rays. CT scans have isolated a subgroup of autistic children with enlarged ventricles and MRI has isolated a subgroup of autistic adults with hypoplasia of the cerebellum vermis.

This damage is consistent with destruction by heat and burn but it also points to failure of tissue in the brain itself to generate in growth to full maturity. It is inviting to believe that this was space naturally made for tissue in the skull cavity that simply never developed. In this explanation the tissue neither developed nor grew to its expected size and maturity; because the germination of budding cells was destroyed. This need not be a particularly given area. Instead it might be the result of the absence of spread or scattered failure to bud and mature all kinds of specific cells.

That growing cells do not fill the brain pan of the skull suggests that the building process is limited to brain tissue and only deep inside the brain at that. It supports the idea that the destruction starts early and at least partly, with the germinating cells which theoretically could stop all cell growth. Someway early on ill effects will become noticeable.

The autistic child with enlarged space in its brain tissue seems to present an uncommon picture in autism but they are there. Instead of some kind of changes spread through the entire brain as one would expect if light passes through the brain and is then spread; there are at times gaping ventricles in the brain. How could it be that there is no consistency to it? A possible answer is that heat hit the brain at a particularly critical time, when buds were just starting to develop a special type of cell. An alternative suggestion would be that it was a very large blast of light, or a prolonged series off blasts that killed a large amount of developing cells. Maybe it was a combination. What ever the circumstances, the child was left with incomplete architecture in its brain.

There is another possible explanation for major changes in tissue gain that might increase the brain mass rather than decrease it. That would be scarring of the brain along the passageways of heat transfer when overloaded by light. It could be that tissue damage is so finely dispersed that changes do not appear on the film. Just scarring the brain is enough to set off seizures in some children. About 20 to 40 percent of autistic children, particularly those with an IQ below 50, start to have seizures before reaching adolescence. Seizures are often related to scars in the brain.

Possible hyperserotonemia occurs in 30-50% of autistic persons with no evidence of central 5-HT abnormalities. There are no specific drug therapies for autism that exist. Individual cases of autism have been associated with congenital rubella syndrome, cytomegalic inclusion body disease, phenoylketonuria, and fragile X syndrome.

4 PHOTOGRAPHY & BURSTS OF LIGHT

The invention of photography affected people's common notions of space, time, and light, and also had a major impact on art. Through knowledge gained in the fields of optic, and chemistry, the scientist built a little machine that could create in an instant what it took an experienced artist days and sometimes months to accomplish. The machine's product was a piece of paper that reproduced a single moment from the space of visual reality. It would come to be called appropriately enough a "snap shot. This put a great number of artists out of a job and vaulted another group of them into "rock star" status.

In modern terms a camera is an instrument used for recording images on photographic film. The total amount of light entering a camera is called the exposure. The lens focuses the light onto the film. When there is insufficient light to produce an adequate image, a flashgun may be used to give extra light.

The first successful photograph was made in 1826 by Nicephore Niepce, [1765-1833], a French lithographer. Ten years later Jacques Daguerre [1789-1851] was experimenting with the process that bears his name. Other improvements followed rapidly.

The official announcement of photography was made in Paris on January 7, 1839. The public's imagination soon propelled daguerreotype portraiture throughout the developed world. When exactly the addition of extremely bright light was added to the making of a photograph is not clear. In 1888 George Eastman introduced the famous box camera with its handy roll of negative film and with the promise of cheap and widely available film processing. Since then photography has become the art form of the masses. Before the invention of photography the great majority of painted images were portraits

Photography soon became the main way to commemorate everything from the launching of boats, to the birth of a child. It also developed a new profession, the professional photographer, with his highly specialized camera and its gigantic flash attachment. These units quickly began to test the public's blink and wink responses, neither of which were fast enough. The result was momentary blindness.

At some time in there light and electricity were added to the camera. Electricity jumps from one electrode to another in an arc, or it flows through a filament, now made of tungsten carbon, whose resistance produces a glowing light. Electricity can light your room and warm your haven and also impair your vision.

With the click of a shutter and the flash of magnesium, the camera would record the here and now with stunning accuracy. By the middle of the century, photographs were ubiquitous throughout Europe. America was soon to follow. The flash of light was soon to develop into an electric light called a flashgun. It could create blinding light with a little tube called a flash bulb. Like so many 'modern inventions'; the new picture machine was not well received by everyone. It is true though that others welcomed it. Among all the mechanical poisons that this terrible nineteen century has poured upon men, lamented John Ruskin, it has given us one antidote, the Daguerreotype.

The camera had an immediate effect on the world of art. The photographer soon took over this trade leaving the artist to consider his fate. The urge to record the visible world hastened the invention of photography. It was a discovery that challenged the process of observation and consequently painting. Not only did the camera undermine the reality of the painted image, it also quickly created a new art form, photography.

The invention of the camera was one of the forces impelling painting toward a more realistic and detached style of expression in art. This match up of renditions of the fleeting iimage of the passing moment was best found in the comparisons of the Mathew Brady photographs done in the battlefields of the Civil War and the painted rendition of Custer's Last Stand which occurred about 12 years later but was not photographed. One is a poor and glorified effort at reconstruction of the fleeting moments, and the other, grim reality.

A review of photography from the early 19th century until 1895, finds all of the research and activity of both the development of the science of reproducing real life pictures and the chemical and paper to store them on, was done in Europe. The greater portion of the work was done in England, France, and Sweden. The introduction of the camera was more limited to France and England. What is most interesting about this for the reviewer is that the first photographic system to be successful on the market, was the

Daguerreotype which became a great success in portraiture throughout the developed world. This was the work of Louis-Jacques Daguerre [1789-1853] French artist and inventor. He invented the first practicable photographic process made public in 1839.

The camera quickly came to America when, at the age of 80, Samuel F. B. Morse built his own photographic camera in 1839. He worked from specifications given to him by Daguerre. whom he had met in Paris.

Just a short time after photography appeared, photographers co-opted use of bright light and invented the flash bulb. From the beginning there was an effort to develop something like modern flash bulbs and flood lights causing a plethora of photons that have bathed the photographers world every since. Strangely the people with the cameras were not the targets of all the light. It was not long after that when people were introduced to great bursts of light. Those who were to be photographed were often coached to keep their eyes open or chastised because a previous picture was a failure because their eyes were closed. The amount or dose of light and the type of light or the make up the light received governed the total heat delivered.

Surely the light flash created by an atomic bomb explosion is markedly different from a photographers flash bulb. The number of pictures, that is to say the number of doses must be important. Since photography began picture taking, for instance, the number of portraits in organized settings has spiraled in the numbers of photos taken.

Babies are a favorite and somewhat defenseless target. It was not long before photographers developed an expertise for lighting. This process which early on demanded two individuals, one to set off the light and anther to go under a cape like blanket to snap the picture. All of this had to be done without exposing the film at the wrong time. Added to this was often repeated direction to the subject 'do not move.' This cumbersome system was then replaced by a single unit with a camera and a 'flash bulb' built around a reflector. These units were sure to supply tremendous amounts of light. It is now not unusual to see those who are followed by the press to be wearing sun glasses. Apparently this helps.

Developing the modern camera was then a fascinating series of events that were closely related. The nation that introduced photography also introduced the photographic portrait to the world, thereby eliminating painted portraiture; the job of artists that had for generations helped to keep the starving artist alive. Then, in what seems to be timely but discouraging fashion, the same locale that introduced the camera, may have discovered autism.

Everyone who has had their picture taken by someone with the modern equipment, has probably had a confrontation with the blinding flash of light that comes with such a happening. Some people complain about it and some seem to let it go unnoticed. Whether they are able to blink or tolerate the blast of light is anybody's guess. The fact that you react to the light means that the light is already in the back of your head and spreading out through the brain. It has passed the cornea very easily. Of course lighting has changed over the past century, but even the newest lighting systems bring light through the cornea or they would not work.

5 BACKGROUND LIGHT

Newborn and infant children are considered here. That is because especially large amounts of concentrated light are used with "flash bulbs" on newborns and infants, sometimes more than once and sometimes in series. This of course means that heat is being thrust into the brains of vulnerable, fragile, and complex developing brains. How much heat is delivered to the baby's brain is unknown. The dose of concentrated light focused in the eye is of course, dependent on the source and repetition.

The human eye has been been adjusted to everyday light over a period of millions of years. The amount of light that came through the visual system of early apes, and on backward through lemurs and so on, was probably limited in some way because of glare. and at the same time rationed by need. The iris can cut down the amount of light entering the eye. There is also a facial muscle ability called squint. To reduce glare, there is a factor of fatigue of the facial muscles. Even though you cannot tire the eyes themselves, the muscles of the face can tire. Also, there is the problem of overload of light which leaves us blind for short periods of time if we are lucky.

Light for all of us is additive. If there is background light it must be added to the product of a flashbulb. In the surroundings of the infant there is almost continuous background lighting such as florescent lights that represent a baseline of light for the human brain to deal with. It is a form of augmentation that is present now almost anywhere. Back ground light is often left on 24 hours a day in homes and public places, factories, and highways. It remains lit year round for safety. For most of us it is light unnoticed. In parking lots at night; the light is rated for protection so it is relatively bright. In schools the lighting is often very bright. Hospitals are particularly well lit. Surgery suites are extremely bright.

The main thing to remember about background light is that it is everywhere, day or night. It acts in more than one way. It is a baseline amount of light to any other light used in its presence. It is present before adding a load of light from photographic flash bulbs. It would be quite a challenge to the stores of energy reserves for a newborn if it were photographed repeatedly.

Much of background lighting is sometimes dimmed down. Especially in casual places where people eat or get out for rest and relaxation. If it is not too bright it may work to keep the iris of the eye dilated and this increases the amount of light entering the eye. In that setting the addition of a flash bulb burst could easily create a photon overload with a period of blindness.

Flash bulbs and the like represent gigantic bursts of light forced into the eyes of the individual often times by being photographed. The photographic camera entered the world sometime after 1839. That it sometimes would need added amounts of light was noted after that.

There is little doubt that the world of photography has taken its place in the modern setting. Some people have moved on from separate or single pictures of their children, to entire albums of photos and now continuous visual recording of their children. All of this can be, and often is, done in bright light.

Bright light, flash bulbs, glare in the desert sun, atomic explosions, and electrical bursts called lightning all can cause visual loss that has the potential to be permanent. Add to that, just looking straight into the sun can leave someone frighteningly without sight. The question is, can light damage and destroy parts of, or all of, the human brain during infancy?

A basic and continuing threat to the human eye is the modern photographic camera. These units come with light augmentation that produces brilliant bursts of light not often sustained but capable of causing short periods of visual impairment in anybody.

6 THE IMPORTANCE OF VISION

One hundred and seventy years ago Abraham Lincoln read law books by candle light, on his way to self education. Now we are surrounded by all kinds of light, mostly from the sun, but added to by a steady increase of man made electrical power, all of it as handy as the flick of a switch. Thus the increase in background light. That was before power lights and autism.

Autism is a condition characterized by a preoccupation with fantasy and a lack of concern for reality. An early sign of autism is indifference to those who give care; an infant may not respond to affection or being picked up. There may be little or no interest in learning to eat, use the toilet, or speak, though there is no difficulty in walking. And yet they are so promising. Such excellent memory and high level of intelligence, can be in a child who has no apparent concern or desire to interact with those around him.

Change such as rearranging furniture, is upsetting to them. It would appear that their perception of the everyday world is distorted and perhaps frightening, so that they seek protection in that which is familiar. Of all our senses to be able to see is the most precious to many of us. It is very difficult to carry out our human actions without it.

Thus, vision is, for man, an extremely important sense. Maybe the most important of all. The eyes of primates periodically evolved to a new level of acuity and color perception and this improvement goaded the brain to further enlargement in order to successfully process the new level of information provided by the streams of protons the eyes were receiving. Thus, at times the growth of the brain in turn propelled further development in vision. Single lens eyes like ours are associated with the need to see clearly into the distance to detect the presence of both prey and predator, and all vertebrates have them.

Based on the above information it appears that the human visual system was developed over a long period of time to gather as much light as possible from the environment on a more or less constant basis. This light creates images for self defense, food gathering and pleasure.

Light constitutes energy, movement and heat; all in one particle. Vision is so important to homo sapien that the stimulus of light is allowed to travel into and through the entire brain itself. Those particles of light then reverberate and scatter throughout the brain to create the image of the fleeting moment. Light is the only stimulus of the five senses that enters into the brain. It not only enters the brain; it enters the brain at the iris of the eye and crosses through the entire brain to its posterior lobes. It then spreads out through the brain in order to reach neurons that must digest its meaning and put it all together to keep the image of our surroundings up to date. Even though it is extremely fast there is a lag time that is measurable, and can be fooled.

The human eye is the primary system in keeping mankind connected to the real world. Sound is notoriously hard to locate but because of vision one can pick up the signs of noise making actions. Human beings have remarkable color vision, second only to birds, and some insects in the range of its spectrum, and our brains are very large. Because we are far from understanding how the cortex of the brain itself works, many of the answers to the questions about vision clearly lie in the future; if indeed they can ever be fully pinned down. Nonetheless, there is considerable agreement among both vision specialists and evolutionary biologists that the human brain and human eyes developed in tandem. That is important in autism because it explains the importance, not only of our field of vision, but also how closely the rest of the brain is connected to the entire body of brain tissue. This connection not only receives signals from the visual cortex; it also passes messages on that penetrate the rest of the brain.

The visual field of a human being, who is awake, keeps constant contact with its surroundings. The normal brain undergoes being altered and updated by messages it accepts in the form of photons. They usually come in amounts that the brain can acquire without difficulty, but in the autistic child messages seem to be either not delivered properly or sometimes not received at all. The visual tissue in the posterior lobes take up 20% of the capacity of the brain. One fifth of our brain in dedicated to vision.

7 THE EYE

The eye is the organ of sight. As light rays enter the eye through the pupil they are focused by the cornea, and lens to form an image on the retina. The main part of the brain that handles vision is in the posterior area known as the occipital lobes. This area is connected to the rest of the brain by neural pathways, that take the stimulus from the visual lobes out into the rest of the brain where it is coordinated in order to create an image of the world around us.

The eyes of primates periodically evolved to a new level of acuity and color perception and this improvement goaded the brain to further enlargement in order to successfully process the new level of information provided by the streams of photons the eyes were receiving. Single lens eyes are associated with the need to see clearly into the distance to detect the presence of both prey and predator, and all vertebrates have them. Thus, at times the growth of the brain in turn propelled further development in vision.

The human eye is a direct outgrowth of the brain. The curved transparent cornea of the vertebrate eye behaves as a fixed lens that guides the streaming photons toward the retina behind it. The cornea is the transparent tissue constituting the anterior sixth of the eye. It is the chief refractory structure of the eye. Light strikes the cornea, the clear front window of the eye, which transmits it to the transparent lens where the light rays are further focused into the retina, the nerve layer at the back of the eye.

The cornea acts to gather light into the lens of the eye by refraction. Refraction is the deflection of a ray of light when it passes from one medium into another of different optic density, in this case, passing from a rarer to a denser medium while being bent toward a perpendicular line. We see the light reflected toward us due to our cornea which acts as a lens and gathers as much light as it can. The cornea can gather more light than is good for us.

After thousands of years of evolution the lens has become primary to our eye. There are differences between creatures that have a single lens eye like our own, and those who have compound eyes. Single lens eyes are associated with the need to see clearly into the distance to detect the presence of both prey and predator, and all vertebrates have them. As the eye developed it became able to detect motion, including direction, and at the highest level, eyes can form images, although the ability to do that varies greatly among different species of mammals. It is crucial to understand, however, that even we humans do not see objects. What we see is the light they reflect. The human eye is built to see and gather reflected light.

Light carried from the eye to the brain on the optic nerve. The optic nerve travels in a passage way just under the upper three quarters of the cerebral cortex. In traveling from the rods and cones to the occipital cortex, a nerve impulse must pass through three neurons. The first has its cell body in the inner nuclear layer of the retina; the second is the ganglion cell of the retina; the third is a neuron with its cell body in the thalmus. It consists chiefly of coarse myelinated fibers which arise in the ganglionic layer of the retina. In mammal studies the optic nerve may contain up to a million nerve fibers, connecting the the sensory cells of the retina to the optical centers in the brain. The majority are third neurons on the visual pathway. During embryological development the optic stalk is converted into the optic nerve by the obliteration of its cavity and the growth of nerve fibers into it.

Most of the fibers grow backward into the optic stalk from nerve cells from the retina, but some extend in the opposite direction and are derived from nerve cells in the brain. For the effects of light, it is a straight shot to the posterior lobe of the brain. The axons of the pigmented nerve cells leave its upper surface, and run laterally through to the geniculocalcarine-fasciculus.

Behind the chiasma the fibers grow backward as the optic tracts to the thalami the mid-brain. The fibers then pass through the posterior and mid section of the brain to terminate in the visual cortex or area striata [area 17] in the immediate neighborhood of the calcarine fissure. Associated fibers connect this area with other regions of the cortex.

Most of the fibers of the optic tract terminate in the a body of fibers called the geniculate body. These are white cells. White matter and brain cells of that color were thought to be insulation and nothing else for many years. It is insulation but it is also an area of the brain that comprises millions of the axons. It has been described as a membrane wrapped around axons, like electrical tape to insulate them. The system carries information between neurons in distant areas of the brain.

In this circumstance it is important to know that the sheath is white because it is high in fat. The importance being that fat burns. While the sheath may be injured by the heat of a burst of high intensity light, it is at least some protection. For the new born, there is no protection at all. The fibers of the optic nerve receive their medullary sheaths about the 10th week after birth. Nerve cells with no protective sheath are then vulnerable to bursts of high intensity heat and it also leaves other enormous numbers of nerve cells in the brain vulnerable to damage if their surrounding cells are overheated. During the ten week period without a medullary sheath the fibers of the optic nerve are vulnerable large bursts of light with their heat, energy, and momentum, breaking down their cellular mechanisms, damaging their cell walls and easily passing the effects of light to other brain cells around them. Both temporal and spatial summation would probably occur because of the great number of photos that are taken now.

It is not just the optic nerve and its pathways that are vulnerable. It has already been pointed out that, malfunctioning or damaged white matter is involved in multiple sclerosis, Alzheimers disease, epilepsy, and perhaps mental illness. The eye is vulnerable outside the cranium as well because "All of the layers of the retina are completed by the eighth month of fetal life." It is clear the the system including the optic nerve can carry more light than is good for us.

This passage begins in the eye and outside of the skull and ends in the occipital cortex of the brain inside the skull. Once the light passes into the skull it is in the cranium, the bones of the head collectively. In a more limited sense, the neurocranium, the bony brain case containing the brain, and excluding the bones of the face. The heat, energy and momentum of light of a large burst of intense light would then come to a halt in the visual cortex. Even though the brain is very well circulated by blood almost directly from the heart; it is very difficult for heat that has entered the brain tissue; for any tissue to divest itself of the heat and in some way act to remove it from the brain. Light travels at such a high rate of speed, there is no easy way for brain tissue to dodge or smother the effects of it.

When the human brain is framing its understanding of reality, not all of the information it considers is in the posterior area of the cerebral cortex. Some of it is sent to the anterior brain. For this reason a large burst of high intensity light that enters the brain will spray heat, energy and movement, all over the brain. The brain will inhale it because the image is subject to constant readjustment from information in several areas. The time involved is very short in duration. That is made clear by the human ability to view an automobile as it passes someone standing near by. The visualization that the individual pictures in his mind, adds understanding of color, size, shape, motion and other factors. These measures of our environment have been used over the centuries to see everything from danger to food. The result of the processing of incoming signals being analyzed, compared, and sent back and forth for corrections before being registered is the construction of the image that the individual finally sees.

The anatomy of the pathway for light in the human brain makes the brain vulnerable for extreme amounts of photons when ever a burst of high intensity light is exposed to the eye.

8 THE BLINK REFLEX

People have a light reflex which helps to dampen extremely bright light. Newborns may not have much of a light reflex, that is to say babies may not be able to block sudden bursts of tremendous light very well. This would seem to leave them at the mercy of flash bulbs.

It is a disturbing fact that when you see the blast of enormous light from a flash bulb on a photographer's camera; the light itself has already traversed your cornea, lens, the retina, the optic nerves, the posterior lobes of the brain, and and scattered into the far regions of the brain. Light travels faster than you can think. Light is the only stimulus of the five senses that enters into the brain. It crosses through the brain to the visual lobe and then spreads out into the brain. Light is the basis of our personal protection system.

We can suffer from an overload of light. In order to defend ourselves from an overload of photons the brain has automatic reflexes that can limit light exposure. Some of this blocking is about the same as common sense. Looking directly into the sun is not only unprofitable but also quite uncomfortable. It is one of those things most people just do not want to do.

To blink is to close and open the eye rapidly and is an involuntary act by which tears are spread over the conjunctiva, keeping it moist. The blinking reflex can be a closing of the eyelids caused by the exposure to bright light, by an attention shift, or by tearing. This is always to late to shut the first flash into the brain. The blink of an eye is very quick but, light is faster. The burst of light generated and delivered in your face can easily break the barrier of the blink or wink system. Almost anyone who has been photographed by a modern camera with a flash attachment will tell you a story of being blinded for a time.

The wink reflex is a general term for closure of the eyelid caused by any stimulus. The visual orbicularis reflex is a contraction of the orbicularis oculi muscle caused by a sudden visual stimulus and causes the eyelids to close when the retina is exposed to light. The pupillary reflex is the change in the size of the pupil as the muscle of the iris contracts or relaxes, responding to altered light intensity or to changed fixation point.

The corneal reflex is carried out by touching the cornea with a wisp of cotton which causes bilateral blinking of the eyelids. The ciliospinal reflex results when pinching the skin of the back of the neck causing pupillary dilatation.

If you assume that these reflexes work immediately on birth they should protect the eye of the baby from the minute it is born but protection in anyone, infant or adult is always relative and will always be altered by things like progress of development etc. For instance, a diminished or absent reflex indicates malfunction of one or more components of the arc or absence of facilitator influences from above. For the newborn a general weakness from a difficult labor, or drugs used during during labor might be a good place to start looking for negative interference in absent reflexes in a newborn.

The tiny nerve system is organized so that it can fire without being told to do so. That is because vision is extremely important and sometimes there is no room for the conscious mind to take part. In fact some people are so taken off guard and unaware that the blink reflex doesn't have time to fire before the threat hits. When that occurs the individual involved is overwhelmed with what may appear to be a white wall. It can be blinding; at least for a period of time.

Visual threat is blinking in response to a hand moving suddenly toward the eyes; such a response becomes consistent in infants after two months of age. This means of course that newborns and babies up to two months of age may have little or no blink protection from bright bursts of light. When you add to this the absence of the nerve's myelin-sheath for the same period or longer; it is clear just how little protection the newborn has from large bursts of intense light and how potentially dangerous that much heat is to neurons that have no protective layer. Not only is there potential to break down the membrane of the cell walls: there is as well the potential of cells joining and passing eletro-magnetic messages across cell walls transferring messages to other pathways as in synesthesia. Synesthesia occurs when a stimulus of one organ channel delivers its image to another organ. If this happens to the average individual they report it to their physician. One can only guess as to how an autistic child might take such an experience.

In the situation in which the individual is photographed multiple times; does the reflex become unable to respond? That is the factor of individual fatigue. Is the newborn child, tired when light exposure takes place? Is one flash enough to cripple the brain? Can the reflex become refractory? Of course.

The word refractory means to be resistant, unresponsive, unmanageable, obstinate, or stubborn. The refractory period is the time following the stimulation during which a nerve or muscle remains unresponsive to a second stimulus. The absolute refractory period is that during which there is no response to any stimulus.

The relative refractory period is that during which the response can be elicited only if the stimulus is very strong. There are factors in the sequence that can effect the quality of the reflex. If the newborn is delivered with little reserve substantive energy, such as carbohydrates, or his eyes have been stimulated multiple times, the light reflex could be exhausted. For the corneal reflex in a child the refractory period could spell a fatigued, overwhelmed, and unresponsive system. Newborn babies are often subjected to flash bulbs quite early, and quite often.

For the average person blocking some light is an everyday activity. The human brain is able to block some of the light on the green and yellow wavelengths, enabling us to perceive red which has a shorter wavelength that is often invisible to us as in infrared red light. As we get older the entire system slows and it appears to be more difficult to work for the victim.

9 BRIGHT LIGHT AND BLINDNESS

There have been events in the past in which light was the key factor in blindness. The record of these events reaches back into the distant past more because of the importance of people who lost there sight. In so far as their exposure to light, the cases range from ignorance of the danger involved with too much light, to self inflicted enormous exposures of direct sunlight. The first recorded very foolish mistake was made by a genius.

These cases are all similar in that the victims were mostly adults except the children at Hiroshima and Nagasaki. None of the individuals were known to be newborns, and in one case the visual loss was due to ignorance or negligence. Every case demonstrates the fact that 'blinding light' is a real thing and it is destructive.

Probably the best known episode of blindness in history is that of Galileo the mathematician and great believer in "the experiment." In 1608 two lens makers managed to notice the effectiveness of a weak convex lens held at arms length combined with a strong concave lens near the eye. Galileo was technically skilled with a gift of improvisation. After hearing of the development of the telescope, Galileo made one on his own. By 1609 he had devised a telescope that magnified 8 times and had improved this to 20 times by the end of the year. He immediately began to study the stars. He looked at sunspots and permanently damaged his eyes.

After publishing this in 1632 he was arraigned before the Inquisition and almost burned at the stake. Instead he was compelled, on pain of death to recant that the earth went round the sun. With four years of his life left to live, his sight failed and his stargazing ended. Too much sun.

His personal trouble began when he started his study of the sun. By magnifying sunlight he had increased the number of photons entering his eye spectacularly. It is important to remember that the human eye is basically organized to gather the greatest amount of light in the visual field and funnel it into the retina. That alone is a powerful focus set up but when Galileo added to that a ten power telescope pointed directly at the sun, it is no wonder that he lost his vision. This load of photons would have passed whatever protection comes from the blink reflex. That he looked straight into the sun long enough to study 'sunspots,' and make sense of them, says a lot about the amount of exposure time he must have gone through. The argument probably could be made that corneal damage or damage to the general surface of the eye was the cause but, the man was left blind. It seems obvious that when a tremendous load of light hits tissue it is likely that there will be a change in the tissue.

There have been circumstances that created extreme light or too much light in a flash. In 1945 the first atomic bomb was set off creating an enormous explosion. With this monumental boom came a sudden, and tremendous burst of white light instantaneously. The flash was so bright and yet so sustained that people were said to have been made blind.

The observations of an expert pertain. "Suddenly at 5:00 A.M. while I was looking in the opposite direction, from O. [ground zero] the night was transferred into a brilliance exceeding that of day light and a wave of heat swept over us. Although my eyes had been opened only a fraction of a second; I was temporarily blinded. We lost no time getting flat against the top of the mountain. Ninety seconds later [remember we were 18 miles away], the air rushed at us and we heard a terrible e blast. Then the blast struck the mountain on either side, and that was echoed as loud as the loudest thunder for several seconds there after.

In the series of atomic bomb explosions that were carried out during WWII, the visual loss was said to be temporary in most but exactly how much permanent blindness resulted is not known. A very similar condition can be created by looking at the sun to long as seen above.

Welders can get a painful condition called 'arc eye.' While caused by bright light, the welder's flash is of longer duration and emits U.V. ultraviolet light rays that can effect the cornea permanently. Welding exposes the welder to the use of long periods of ultraviolet light in a rather concentrated form. This is a craft that can, if the worker is not protected against the specific light of the arc, can lead to blindness. So dangerous is the light of the arc, people entering the area of its use, are advised not to look at the arc or else get protective glasses. Ultraviolet light is just a portion of white light. Flash blindness, in contrast, can be caused by a single very brief exposure which over saturates the retina, and is not usually accompanied by reports of pain.

The human brain is magnificent in its size and complexity, but it is at the same time a very fragile electrical wiring system that works exceedingly fast.

It is vulnerable. A treatment program for psychiatric patients was started in the mid 20^{th,} century. Known as electro-shock-therapy or ECT. Its use became quite common in the management of certain types of patients. Whether it was good for the patients is still being argued; but there is no doubt that under direct bolts of electricity some brain cells ceased to work normally. This was documented by periods of amnesia after the treatments. Some of this memory loss was recovered but not all. One thing is sure. We are left with clear evidence of destruction or distortion of the brain cells; simply by overloading brain cells with electrons.

10 FLASH BLINDNESS & LASER

A laser is a device that can concentrate high energy into an intense narrow beam of nondivergent monochromatic radiation. Lasers are used in several sorts of exacting work including surgery and printing. These devices are handled with care. They are a light source that is understood to be dangerous.

Flash blindness is visual impairment during and following exposure to a light flash of extremely high intensity. A flash in this paper is a sudden and brief burst of light and heat. Light is by definition heat, energy and movement. This phenomenon is leveraged [by the military] in nonlethal weapons such as flash grenades and laser dazzlers. It may last for a few seconds or a few minutes. For example, in every day life the subject of a photograph can cause temporary flash blindness. The bright light overwhelms the eye and only gradually fades. A bright spot or spots, may be seen for many minutes.

Flash blinding is caused by bleaching [over-saturation] of the retinal pigment. As the pigment returns to normal, so to does sight. In daylight the eye's pupil constricts, thus reducing the amount of light entering after the flash. At night, the dark adapted pupil is wide open so flash blindness has a greater effect and lasts for a longer time.

The bright initial flash of a nuclear weapon is the first indication of an nuclear explosion, traveling faster than the blast wave or sound wave. "A one megaton explosion can cause flash blindness at distances as great as 13 miles on a clear day and 53 miles on a clear night. If this intensity is great enough, a permanent retinal burn will result." The reader should take note the writer here described the injury as a burn. The values are based on adults.

Some sources, such as NATO, and the U.S. Department of Defense state that flash blindness can be temporary or permanent. Other sources restrict the use of the word for temporary, reversible vision loss. There are in order of increasing, dazzle, after image formation, flash blindness, and irreversible damage. The U.S. Federal Aviation Administration in order 7400.21 defines it as a generally temporary visual interference affect that persists after the source of the illumination has ceased. Other sources restrict the word to temporary, reversible vision loss. Because there appears to be no consensus definition, one should be especially clear about which sense of the phrase is meant For example, using the phrase [temporary flash blindness] when discussing everyday flash photography, emphasizes that the condition will fade away with out effect.

Because vision loss is sudden and takes time to recover, flash blindness can be hazardous. At some sporting events such as figure skating, fans are cautioned to not use flash photography so as to avoid distracting the athletes. In aviation pilots are trained to recover from bright nearby lightning flashes. Also in aviation, there is concern about lasers and bright searchlights causing temporary flash blindness and other distracting effects, in pilots who are in critical phases of flight such as approach and landing.

In the modern day work force it is probably electricians who experience accidental exposure to accidental flash light more than anyone else. This usually occurs when there is a breaking of a hot [active] line of electricity. The result is grounding of the electricity. When the line disconnects the electricity arcs and at that point a burst of light appears. This light is usually blue and can be seen as anywhere from quite bright to only slight. The flash can make some noise. The event can leave the individual involved with temporary visual loss and some pain in the head.

It is unclear whether pain is directly associated with the flash blindness. Reaction to flash blindness can be discomforting and disorienting. The retina has no pain receptors, so reports of pain might be due to more psychological reactions mixed with facial muscular reaction. That the individual involved has real pain is sure.

Commercially available photographic flash units for cameras were developed over a century ago so that photography could be performed under reduced light levels A study was done on "Phototoxic effects of commercial photographic flash lamp on rat eyes. They are generally considered to be safe because of their extremely short flash duration. However, the well known after images suggest that they do have a long lasting effect on the retina, and the instruction manuals for the flash units warn users of the possibility of injury by firing the flash close to the eye. Close to the eye means more heat.

However very few studies have been done to examine the photo toxicity of such flash units for cameras. The aim of this study was to determine whether flashes from commercially available photographic flash lamps can damage ocular tissue. The eyes of rats were exposed to different numbers of flashes from a commercially available photographic flash unit, and both morphological and physiological techniques were used to assess the corneas and the retina.

The study above is interesting and useful but it does not seem to apply to the needs for this hypothesis in two ways. First, the tissues of the animals in the study group were specifically taken to examine changes in the retina. The findings seem to be consistent with the aims of the study group. But, there is no information about the brain tissue itself. Second, the age of the animals, or their stage of maturity is not clear. That is to say, were they babies or adults or either? Also it would have been good to know if the behavior of the animals during the period of receiving so much light.

A very important fact is to be taken from flash blindness. Adult human beings can be permanently blinded by light.

11 THE SUNBURN MODEL & MACULA LUTEA

The model for destruction of brain tissue by the heat of the sun is sunburn or the destruction of skin by sunlight. In both sunburn and autism, whether damage to skin or damage to the brain, it is large doses of sunlight that cause the injury.

We have always been vulnerable to extremely bright light. We know this from long experience with everything from the glare of glass to lightning bolts. Mankind has suffered physical injuries due to sunlight, by leaving their babies in the sun, only to find them sunburned, and travelers on "sun drenched" deserts who acquire blindness from the constant sunlight. We have known for years that exposure to brief but intense doses of light can cause short periods of blindness. A similar phenomenon can occur when people go from a darkened space such as a theater out to bright daylight. In that condition the brain must switch from using dark sensitive rods in the eye to color sensitive cones, a process which can take several seconds. Most people will stop until the temporary visual loss corrects.

There are other glaring examples of the effects of destructive actions that light can have on human tissues. One of the most common effects of repeated doses of light on skin tissue is when sunburn creates total death of layers of skin and its contiguous tissue. Sunburn is a model for brain damage by light, even though the light involved is operating in two different environments. Both injuries are the same in type being thermal burns.

Burns from ultraviolet rays, such as sunburn, cause delayed erythema [redness] and tenderness on exposed areas of the skin. They begin with erythema and swelling, possibly followed by deep or superficial blisters and other signs of damage that depend on the severity of the burn.

One consequence of this is the synthesis of different proteins and enzymes. The effects of these proteins lead to dilation of cutaneous blood vessels and recruitment of inflammatory cells. The warmth of a sunburn generally stems from increased blood flow to the exposed
area.

Apparently there are no measurements of sunburned skin but studied consideration has led experts to suspect that even though the burned skin seems much warmer, it would still be close to 98.6 degrees Fahrenheit. Any slight elevation in temperature would be of an inflammatory response generated by the processes induced by ultraviolet radiation. Sunburn takes place in an open environment; where penetration of photons breaks tiny holes in a tough surface [the skin] and swells the local cells enough that they come apart and die.

The macula lutea or macula retina is an oval area of the sensory retina. It is 3 by 5 mm in area, temporal to the optic disk corresponding to the posterior pole of the eye; at its center is the central fovea, which contains only retinal cones and, it is very close to the brain. Known as the fovea there is a depression in the center of the macula that contains no blood vessels. Disease in that area has been called maculopathy, solar maculopathy, electric retinopathy, and solar retinopathy.

Flash here means a sudden and brief burst of light or heat. A sudden flash of light is a burst of heat; they are one and the same. When intense light passes the macula, the brain is vulnerable. Light can increase or expand the unicellular pressure of the walls of the pathways of neurons. It can breakdown these cells and release ions in the brain that destroy other cells or pieces of DNA. It could involve the entire brain because sunlight always has generalized connections throughout the brain.

There is an example of sunlight heating human nerve tissue in the visual system. Called photoretinopathy or photoretinitis, it is a macular burn from excessive exposure to sunlight or other intense light [for example the flash of a short circuit] characterized subjectively by reduced visual acuity.

The brain is in a closed environment, the skull. It is a more individual cellular environment than the skin. Skin is tough and built to resist all sorts of weather. Even though skin is damaged by sunlight, it is a target that is out in the open air and able to deal with the heat of light simply because the surrounding air is usually lower in temperature than the body. Added to that there is melanin which, given time, resists sunlight. The outdoors are not only open air with a lower temperature, much of the time there is a breeze or some movement of the air around the sunburned.

The neuron of the brain is an all or nothing, one way element. The cells of the retina are connected in such a way that a strong impulse will go to the brain.

The signal that goes to the brain consists of impulses running along axons that in affect, break the visual field into a series of bright and dark dots. These signals arrive at the primary visual cortex at the back of the brain. The signals involved here are running along the axons and carrying messages made of broken down series of bright and dark dots. Sometimes the receiving cells sees dark dots tilted at a 45 degree angles others have bright edges. This all works to create a very fragile system. To carry on, the signals then feed into a set of cells in one particular layer of the visual cortex, all so located in the back of the brain. The output from these cells, in turn, is passed on to other cells, perhaps in other parts of the brain for further integration. Other signals are following the chain upward to ever more specialized neurons.

Kirchhoffs showed that objects that are good emitters are also good absorbers. Eyes are good absorbers of heat, energy and momentum, as well as good emitters. That is when it is in the body as a whole. But, when [heat, energy and momentum,] is forced into the brain in a large burst of intense light, the mass of photons involved will burn, distort, and destroy tissue along the neural pathways.

The eye is easily entered. Large numbers of photons streaming into the brain and scattering out through its tissue are quite similar to sunburn except they are inducing macular retinitis disease. The human body is a good absorber of ultraviolet light. Large amounts of light energy and heat penetrating the skin cause sunburn by swelling the skin tissue which breaks the skin, releasing water, and electrolytes.

When it comes to sun exposure what you can't see will hurt you. The spectrum of natural sunlight contains among other things, ultraviolet light [UV] photons. These photons are shorter in wavelength and higher in energy than visible light. The longer wave-length UVA high energy photons penetrate the deeper layers of the skin, where they generate free radicals and can damage your DNA. It is these free radicals loose in the brain after a hit by a large burst of light that account for some of the damage and or death of cells local to the neural pathway, and explain at least some of any distant tissue destruction.

Because the skull is closed there is no simple way for heat of light to escape. The victims of large amounts of light entering the brain have no built in system to unload a blast of heat. The temperature around a photon mass will raise and lower as the photons disperse. In a closed environment, like the skull, the heat and energy will have no direct loss to open air. Instead, it will be trapped along the edge of the neural pathways and the heat will expand and disperse throughout the brain. In that circumstance they can burn, damage, or destroy, neural pathways and tissue not just in juxtaposition to neurons but other local cells. Any atoms and molecules released at that time; will breakdown other substantive parts of surrounding cells and their atoms and molecules. Those particles will carry on destroying other tissue until the heat is gone.

Brain tissue is defenseless in comparison to skin because much of it has no thick layer of keratin. Brain tissue is then very likely to absorb light but with the almost singular characteristic of having no pain receptors. Because there are no pain receptors in the brain tissue the individual does not feel the sensation of an injury like a sunburn. In an infant, with a brain that is just beginning to develop, this can be a disaster. There is an indirect factor that helps to control the temperature of the brain and body. That is the blood circulation system, which keeps us at
98.6.

Infection or destruction of the macula of the eye, threatening as it is to the individual's vision, is for this discussion, outside of the skull. Even so, it is an extremely clear and exacting example of what intense light can do to neuron-transmitters and their contiguous tissues inside the eye and at the opening to the brain. It is also important to remember; the accidental flash of a short circuit is hopefully a once in a lifetime experience, whereas baby pictures come in bunches. While this might not destroy much tissue in any one place its exposure would be quite large considering that the injury is in the area of spread that light can travel in the brain.

One of the most discouraging problems for the autistic child is their lack of visual acuity. The visual lobe is the first tissue mass an intense burst of light would reach. Their world is that of shapeless masses.

12 VULNERABILITY

Autism is a disorder that leaves infants in a state in which they are relatively isolated, seemingly from just after birth. These children are certainly disconnected but not simply from people, basically they are are isolated from the world around them. The condition is called "loneness."

Development in biological terms is the series of events occurring in an organism during the change from a fertilized egg to the adult stage. The critical period of fetal [before birth] development is during embryo genesis when the cells are partly finished, yet vulnerable to damage [toxin agent], disrupting the normal pattern of events. Early in development cell groups are delicate and dainty, even frail. Cell walls are weak and and easily broken because they are very thin. Some tissue remains weak into adulthood. This leads to CNS malformations that cause a large number of fetal, neonatal, and infant deaths. It is estimated that 3% of neonates have significant CNS or other systemic malformations. Genetic abnormalities, maternal infection, drugs, and illness account for 40% of malformations, however, the cause in the remaining 60 % is unknown.

Autistic children are on the cusp of being normal; they are at the edge of fitting into society. The damage in their brains seems slight and yet quite pervasive. It acts like a thin layer of discord that traps them. It seems as if their brains were attacked by a limited but poisonous substance at one of the most fragile times of their growth and development; that is just after delivery..

While the newborn is fragile it is also a defenseless being. On its way in the world to be adulthood, it is a bundle of millions of cells of many different types, all of them coded to receive messages that will cause them to develop into complexes of skin and bone mixed with brains, muscles, glands and other tissues. All of the tissues are orchestrated to begin developing at certain times and to be sent on their way by formative cell groups. Protected in the brain many of the message centers are usually safe. However the system that protects them is often not sufficient to control large loads of light that modern living provides.

At the time of the baby's birth; it is still in the formative period which will continue for years. One part of the system is particularly sensitive. This is the reticulate formation. It is a massive but vaguely delimited neural apparatus composed of closely intermingled gray and white matter and extending throughout the central core of the brain-stem and into the diencephalon. The brain tissues of newborns have many twists and turns. When it comes to growth and development, it must be remembered that at the same time this very fragile tissue is constantly changing; it is also developing in size and complexity. Fetal and newborn brain tissue is made particularly fragile and vulnerable because it is quite small and thin, and some of it is made up of tiny buds that are just starting on their way to maturity. This period is further complicated by the tiny bud-like architectural formations of germinating tissues that are coming forth. These germ cell nests are bursting with new cells that fill out and equip organs and parts that will in time complete the brain.

The great vulnerability to the fetus is that any slight or small injury can create an error on the pathway to maturity. This would destroy or distort future tissue growth. Large amounts of light dispersed in the formative dynamic is a risk of distortions, malformations, and twisted or burnt developmental pathways of the cells of the infant's fetal brain and its connections. The end result could be changed shapes, constitutional make-up, and potential limited or confused function.

For the newborn this is a treacherous circumstance. Infancy demands regular and nutritious feedings. When and if fetal and newborn tissues are affected by heat they would be in a rapid developing stage. They are sensitive to the slightest damage which might effect cells during the formative period. Thus any interference with growth can stunt or stop normal cell reproduction, distort normal architecture, and eliminate the usual signals that tell the [base] histilogical cells to stop or start the formation of such things as glands, skeletal parts, neurological precursors, etc.

When flashes of intense light enter the eye and travel through the brain they carry large amounts of increased heat through the nerve system. Among its many effects here on earth, light can destroy or damage human tissue including the neurons and contiguous cells throughout the brain.

It is the areas nearest the nerve pathways that would be most vulnerable to burns as unusual heat appeared. The posterior lobes would be the first target of burn. Light stops there and turns completely around in order to spread out into the brain.

Autistic children are a visual mystery. At times they seem to stare at people with no sign of recognition on their part, however I have seen them run down a hall and turn a corner with out trouble, an action that takes both good vision and agility. Then too, one can spend hours with them and never feel connected. That any burn in the brain is going to effect the victim in someway, there is no doubt. In the case of autism the effects are confusing at best.

13 THE FRAGILE NEURON

In animals, the body cells that detect stimuli are called receptors, and these are often contained within a sense organ. For example the eye is a sense organ within which the retina contains rods and cones which are receptors. Communication by stimuli is through the use of electro-magnetic messages, receptors to effectors.

When struck by a photon, the retina absorbs the light energy and changes shape from 'kinked' to 'straight'. This converts the opsin part of the molecule into an active enzyme, sparking a cascade of reactions that results in the release of a transmitter at the junction between the light-receptor cell and a optic nerve cell. Exposure to light quickly releases the retinal from the opsin.

The retina contains millions of light-sensitive cells, called rods and cones, which convert the image into a pattern of nerve impulses. Information from the two optic nerves is processed in the brain to produce a single coordinated image. Once focused by the cornea and lens a stream of photons can gain access to the brain by simply traveling through the optic nerve. That means a large amount of light in a single dose, can deliver a large amount of heat in an extremely brief period of time.

Light moving at 186,000 miles per second, focused down from the individuals field of view to the width of the operating portion of the optic nerve is asked to carry any number of particles of light and deliver them to many brain cells in the rear of the brain. The light is processed in the retina to some extent and on arrival in the area, the load of light\signals stop. It is then processed again and separated. Some of the light turns 180 degrees in order to travel back into the deep tissues of the entire brain as it spreads and ends its motion. That may be where the greatest damage of the brain occurs. All of this is done almost instantaneously.

Rapid communication and response that is stimuli by light or sound, is essential to an animal's well being. However, the system is so efficient in its effort to catch light and pass it on that it can easily become over loaded. In humans the nerve cells are made of membrane, cytoplasm, nucleus, and long thin fibers termed nerve dendrites and axons. The longest of these, the axons, can be more than a meter in length, and the other, the dendrite, somewhat shorter. It is this very fragile system that we depend on to view the world.

That it might stand up to a burst of intense light, heat, energy, and movement, is questionable. The lens will take almost any number of photons that are delivered to it, and the receptor system of the eye is able to receive and pass on large amounts of light. While we need to see as much as we can take in, which is almost any amount of light we are exposed to, we must protect our eyes and brain lest we are blinded.

There are some limits such as how quickly the lid can be closed and shut off to extremely bright light. In adults for instance, the eye might be late because of modern "flash bulbs." There is only so much information that the brain can process no matter the source. The result of this is any overload of photons is dangerous.

There is another factor that operates constantly to speed up processing. It is the synapse. They are extremely tiny. Synapses use only twenty-nanometers of space in the brain, an area so small that it can only be seen by an electron microscope. Because they are so small messages can cross the synapse almost instantly. However their size and their fragile state also makes them very vulnerable.

Because the appearance of light in the brain creates vision it is clear that the effects of light particles are operating in the brain almost constantly under normal conditions. But it is also clear that the effects of light on those pathways in the brain could be subject to an overload of light which might deter its neurons momentarily or destroy the neurons and the tissue around them. Once delivered inside the body light/heat may work in different ways.

In this way the entire system is made vulnerable to light in almost any amounts. Neurons fire and pass information onward through a chain of cells, while at the same time feedback signals pass down the chain and affect lower cells. This system also sends signals upward on a chain to ever more specialized cells.

14 SAFETY IN LOCATION

The brain is for most of us a very mysterious place. It is the major organ of the central nervous system and control for all the body's voluntary and involuntary activities. It is also responsible for the complexities of thought, memory, emotion, and language. Down under its tough scalp, rests the hard headed bony skull and all of those leather like wrappers, that protect those millions of neurons that are so very fragile. In adults, this complex organ is a mere 3 lb. in weight, containing more that 10 thousand million nerve cells.

Three distinct regions can easily be seen, the brain stem including the medulla oblongata, the cerebellum, and the cerebrum. The medulla oblongata contains centers for the control of respiration, heart beat rate, and the strength or level of blood pressure, and thermo-regularity control, the control of body temperature. Of the three parts of the brain, the medulla oblongata is the most posterior subdivision of the brain stem, immediately continuous with the spinal cord. The organ of control is shielded from light. A burst of high tense light will not bother the area of hindbrain. The symptom group that is to say, pulse, blood pressure, respiration, and temperature, are not bothered by autism for that basic reason.

Overlying the medulla oblongata is the cerebellum which is concerned with coordinating complex muscular processes such as maintaining posture and moving limbs and the control of balance. It is much closer to the pathway of light entering the brain. Unfortunately it shares fibers of message carrying neurons with the cerebrum. Thus, one of the most notable symptoms of autistic children is their lack of response to cuddling. They do not 'mold' to the body of a parent who picks them up to hold or carry them. This lack of interest and ability to form their body to mother, originates in two parts of the brain; the parietal lobe and the cerebellum. Embracing and snuggling take some physical ability that the cerebellum under normal conditions would supply.

15 THE BRAIN

The brain is the part of the central nervous contained in the skull or cranium. The brain is a mass of interconnected nerve cells controlling the anterior part of the central nervous system whose activities it coordinates and controls. The cerebrum [cerebral hemispheres] are outgrowths of the front end of the forebrain which was developed in early vertebrates mainly concerned with the senses. But, in the higher vertebrates especially humans it is greatly developed. It is involved in the integration of all sensory input and motor output, and in thought, emotions, memories, and behavior.

Sensory input arrives in the cerebrum in the form of impulses such as light, from receptors of sense organs such as the retina of the eye. It is of course light sensitive organs like the cones of the retina that suffer the initial blast from intense flash bursts. The entire cerebrum suffers the main thrust of heat when a flash of intense light enters the eye. In direct contrast to the medulla oblongata which seems to take the least of the burn of light because it is shielded by distance from the pathway of light; there are areas of the brain and nerve system that suffer most because they are on the pathway of light.

The prefrontal cortex is an area of the brain involved in higher order decision making. Accordingly it has been found that the frontal lobes are important in regulating complex behavior, the organization and planning of purposeful activities and the coordination of intention with action. Brain lesions of the frontal lobe result in impairment of abstract or complex gnostic and intellectual functions, loss of purposeful behavior, of complex forms of behavior, and perseveration. The frontal lobe is also concerned with eye movements, and papillary changes. The size, location, and extent, of the damage to the frontal lobes determines the type of impairment that will occur. Lesions of these areas result in the impairment of planned, purposeful behavior.

The parietal lobe is the area of the cerebrum between the frontal and occipital lobes. This area contains the somesthetic [sensory] or parietal cortex, which receives messages [intake] from all sensory neurons except those involved with vision. Damage in this area can produce impairment in sensation or parentheses such as numbness, tingling, or heightened sensitivity.

The parietal cortex structure and function of the cutaneous and kinesthetic [action] analyzer provides the basis of motor activity. It is important for discrimination based upon deep pressure sensitivity. A brain lesion of the parietal lobe can cause afferent motor agnosia. That is messages going to the nucleus to be acted on. It can also cause tactile agnosia which are difficulties in [touch] recognition of objects.

Brain lesions of the parietal lobe can set off apraxia. The appearance of apraxia creates an inability to distinguish among objects or to identify objects by touching them. The individual may also be unsure how to use familiar objects. The symptoms outlined here would explain problems of autistic children such as their difficulty molding to their mother's form when being picked up or carried. There is the also the loss of familiarity of touch in the autistic child. The parietal lobe seems to be one of the more safe areas from a large burst of intense life. Two things are working here that could operate against the area which is next to and somewhat connected to the calcarine cortex and it receives messages from all sensory neurons except visual ones.

The temporal lobes process visual recognition, auditory perception, memory, and emotion. Patients with acquired unilateral damage to the right temporal lobe commonly lose acuity for non verbal auditory stimuli such as music. Left temporal lobe injury interferes severely with the recognition , memory, and formation of language. The temporal lobes are connected with the calcarine cortex.

A brain lesion of the occipital lobe area results in inability to remember sequential elements of an act. The past is not forgotten. A brain lesion of the occipital-parietal area may involve visual agnosia, visual alexia, agraphia, acalculia, and aphasia semantic. Visual alexia, also known as word blindness, is characterized by inability to recognize individual letters.

16 THE AMYGDALA

The amygdaloid body is an ovoid mass of gray matter about the size and shape of an almond in the roof of the rostral [toward the front] end of the lateral ventricle.

It is an almond shaped region of the brain adjacent to and closely associated with the cortex covering the uncus [the temple of the head] of the gyrus hippocampi. It links the cortex tissue responsible for conscious thought, with the regions controlling emotions. Also called the amygdaloid nucleus it is a mass of grey matter in the cerebrum located approximately under the tip of the temporal lobe. It is thought to be one of the interconnected and motivational centers of the old brain.

The temporal lobe is a part of the brain related to memory and a variety motor and sensory responses. This places the nucleus in connection to the responses to threats of danger by the "fight or flight response" and survival mechanisms such as emotions and pleasure. The amygdala is involved in the assessment of character in unfamiliar people by using knowledge of past experiences to determine whether a person is, for example, trustworthy or friendly. For example, where the amygdala is damaged, patients are unable to recognize fearful expressions. It is then not surprising that stimulation of certain amygdaloid nuclei can sometimes cause a pattern of rage, escape, punishment, and pain similar to the affective defense pattern elicited by the hypothalamus. It can cause the animal to develop a defensive posture, extend its claws, his spit, and develop wide-open eyes, and dilated pupils. It can cause tonic movements, such as raising the head or bending the body, circling the movements, occasionally clonic, rhythmic movements, and movements associated with taste and eating, such as licking, chewing, and swallowing. Stimulation can also alter respiration, and at other times it can stop all movement. In turn it transmits signals back into the same cortical areas, and others above.

The amygdala is involved in interpreting fear-provoking information and linking it to fear responses. For example, where the amygdala is damaged patients are unable to recognize fearful expressions. The amygdala is involved in assessment of character of unfamiliar people by using knowledge of past experiences to determine whether a person is for example, trustworthy or friendly. Emotionally charged events are more easily recalled than neutral events and in 1996 U.S. researchers demonstrated a link between the amygdala and the memorizing of emotionally loaded images. This is treacherous territory. For sometime now it has been known that some of the most disingenuous people we deal with in life, come across as friendly and accommodating. Those people with damaged amygdalas were found, in a 1998 study, to be unable to make these judgments.

It could be that a burst of high intensity light has caused damage to the neurons and scarification with swelling, that leads to permanent enlargement of tissue. The link between enlargement and damage seems logical. It is important to remember that the amygdala is associated with the reward system of the mind. This area is near the optic nerve, passing through to the visual lobe. Any large burst of intense light has two exposures to the hippocampus. The amygdala sits beneath the cerebrum and near the optic nerves. It has strong connections with the prefrontal lobe of the brain. The prefrontal lobe is the end site of large bursts of intense light that recoil from the visual lobe and travel to the frontal lobe and prefrontal lobe, thus it offers two exposures of light to the amygdala at almost the same time. It makes the amygdala doubly vulnerably to large bursts of intense light because it is anatomically close to the optic nerves and at the same time it is directly connected to the prefrontal lobe.

Autistic children have little joy in life. Their inability to recognize and feel warm around friends, family and surroundings, interferes with relationships and identification. A lesion in the amygdala would increase the characteristic of ambivalence.

17 CHAOS

Chaos is a state of such disorganization that it has no constructive predicates. It is a state in which no causal relationships are operating. The results are random. Such is the case when a large burst of intense light enters the eye, streams down the optic nerve, bounces off of the visual cortex and careens into the brain.

The neural pathways are not hollow conduits. They are instead long threads of nerve tissue and membrane intertwined cords of nerve cells. A nerve is a bundle of nerve cells enclosed in a sheath of connective tissue and transmitting nerve impulses to and from the brain and spinal cord. Each neuron has three parts: a cell body, branching dendrites that receive chemical signals from other neurons, and a tube-like axon that conveys these signals as electrical impulses. The unit of of information is the nerve impulse a traveling wave of chemical and electrical changes involving the membrane of the nerve cell. A substance called a neurotransmitter is the chemical that diffuses across a nerve junctions, [synapses] and thus transmits impulses between nerve cells or nerve cells and effector organs such as a muscle. Noradrenaline is a common neurotransmitter and powerful stuff. This substance and others are able to cross the membrane of the cell partly because of its fine, delicate, and fragile condition.

If a neuron that works at a specific rate is suddenly run over by a tremendous load of electricity, heat and energy, that cell will misfire or be destroyed. It all starts with light. Normally, the receptors in our eyes are sensitive to a small window of the electro-magnetic spectrum: light with wavelengths in the range of about 400 to 800 nm. A nanometer, abbreviated nm, is six orders of magnitude smaller than a millimeter. When packages of light, photons, enter the eye and strike the retina, the energy they contain must be converted via a series of complex steps, into an electrical signal that passes from the retina to the optic nerve and then to the brain. It is the conversion of chemical signals into electrical impulses, that makes the nerve system vulnerable.

There are several destructive physiological reactions that can occur, when a large burst of intense light forces its way onto the neuropathways of the brain. That is because of the make up of sunlight and its velocity. Electromagnetic waves are at anytime oscillating electric and magnetic fields traveling together through space at a speed of 186,000 miles per hour. Light is a form of energy. Visible light is composed of electromagnetic waves. It is a type of electro-magnetic radiation, like X rays or radio waves. All electromagnetic radiation is produced by electric charges which is caused by the effects of oscillating electric and magnetic fields as they travel through space. Electromagnetic radiation is considered to have both wave and particle properties.

Heat is transferred by the movement of particles that possess kinetic energy by conduction, convection, and radiation. The electromagnetic spectrum is a family of waves that include radio waves, infrared radiation, visible light, [white light], ultraviolet radiation, X rays, and gamma rays. All electromagnetic waves can be, reflected, [rebounded] refracted [bent], diffracted, and polarized.

Heat is energy and movement transferred to temperature difference. All types of energy and movement can be given off as heat in the form of radiating electromagnetic waves. Hotter objects emit more energy than colder objects. Energy in biology is the basis of conducting living processes. Heat does not flow spontaneously from a colder to a hotter body. It always flows from a region of higher temperature [heat intensity] to one of lower temperature, Claucius 1888. Any focus of light that meets a surface brings with it heat and can increase the heat of the surface. Thus a difference in temperature between two objects in thermal contact leads to the transfer of energy as heat.

A sudden exposure to a marked change in temperature such as a burst of intense heat, means rupture to the neurons of the brain where ever the light goes. Because the resting temperature in the brain is 98.6 in humans, it is logical that bursts of distinctly hotter waves of light with relatively greater energy would transfer heat, by both conduction and convection to brain tissue.

With movement, heat is able to penetrate all sorts of brain tissue passing through until it hits and divides something, breaks something or loses all of its energy. The heat it creates can burn, distort, maim, bend, melt, kill, and simply destroy, all sorts of things including human tissue. Its effect on a substance may be simply to raise its temperature or cause it to expand, melt, [if a solid] vaporize [if a liquid] or increase its pressure [if a confined gas]. It can carry out all of these actions when large doses of it are allowed to enter the brain in a very short time. Delivered into the brain in powerful bursts, light can overwhelm human tissue. It has the potential to be lethal.

Convection involves the transfer of energy by the movement of fluid particles. Although the concept of energy consisting of particles was revolutionary, it was quickly seized on by Albert Einstein. In his fourth important paper of 1905, Einstein used Planck's theory to explain the photoelectric effect, proposing that when light particles strike the surface of particular metals electrons are necessarily jettisoned. This occurs as part of the scatter of incoming heat in the brain. Basically, particles that are someway separated from one connection, will come to rest in another.

The destructive character of heat delivered in a substantive mass such as the brain would be, at least in part, [convection] as it permeates any of the neurons connected to the passageways into and throughout the brain. With heavy bursts of light or several repetitive bursts of light, heat could do damage to brain tissue in the form of distortion, twisting, with death the result.

Dispersion in physics is a particular property of refraction in which the angle and velocity of waves passing through a dispersion medium depends upon their frequency. Light is dispersed in accordance with Newton's inverse square rule. It is a measure spread.

When visible white light passes through a prism it is split into a spectrum. This occurs because each component frequency of light which corresponds to a color, is refracted by a slightly different angle, and so the light is split into the component frequencies[colors. It is also an indication that some parts of the dispersed light will be hotter than others. This means some tissue in the brain will be burned more than others. Inside the skull dispersed light in large amounts would find it difficult to impossible to stay on the dedicated pathways of neurons. Portions of the light would then seep or fly out into surrounding tissue.

Expansion is the increasing of size of a constant mass of substance, in this case, increasing its temperature [thermal expansion] or its internal pressure. Expansion, induced by the heat increases pressure on the local cells. This is made obvious by swelling, and fluid escaping from broken cells all induced by the heat in sunburn. In either, change like distortion, torsion, swelling and twisting must result. In this circumstance damaged neurons in groups would swell as a body of dead cells and block messages.

The circulation of 98.6 blood in the brain is supplied by relatively large arteries and veins. They do a wonderful job of maintaining near normal temperatures during febrile producing infections of the brain but, a lightning like strike of concentrated light that enters the eye and sizzles throughout the brain is a very different matter. It is clear that the increase in heat does not need to be very large to damage or destroy local cells.

In neurophysiology summation refers to responses attained when two stimuli are applied, neither of which by itself is of sufficient intensity to elicit a response. In this sense, there are two types of summation, temporal and spatial. Either of these can be set off by overheating.

Temporal summation is seen when two successive stimuli, each of them too weak to elicit a response, are applied to the same nerve trunk within .1 to .5 millisecond of each other in which case a response will be evoked because of the enduring character of the local excitation process. Spatial summation is seen when two different afferent nerves which play upon the same reflex center are stimulated either instantaneously or within a short interval [not more than 15 milliseconds] a response even though neither stimulus alone elicit a response. Spatial summation is believed to be the result of additive excitation alterations in the neurons involved. This is referred to as the "central excitation state."

The developmental age of an individual's architecture of the brain is very important to the invasion of heat. The tissue of an infant does not have to be destroyed to become autistic; partial injury will change the outcome. In some parts of the brain developmental change is stopped. Arrested development is the failure of an organism to carry out the normal evolution, stopping at the initial stage of the process.

18 AGNOSIA

The word agnosia has been used in several ways. For this paper an agnosia is a complete or partial inability to recognize and attach meaning in the impression of a sense organ. The concept of agnosia is an inability to interpret sensations and hence to recognize things. Specifically; agnosia means "not knowing," with particular reference to sensory stimuli such as visual agnosia. auditory agnosia, color agnosia, and finger agnosia. In visual agnosia for instance, the individual is able to perceive what ever is in his visual field but is unable to recognize what he is seeing. As a neuropsychologic term agnosia means an uncommon deficit in which an object cannot be identified despite the capacity to identify its tactile [touch] or visual elements. Simply put, "An individual with agnosia is unable to correctly perceive and identify familiar objects."

Agnosias can be receptor site defects caused by lesions in various portions of the cerebrum. The condition can involve any sensory system and is often the result of cortical [brain] damage. The visual lobe is the tissue area that takes the most direct hits of large bursts of high intensity light from the optic nerve, and inability to recognize objects is one of most constant symptoms of autism. Destruction of the sensory association areas greatly reduces the capability of the brain to analyze different characteristics of sensory experiences.

The infant with autism finds himself in a much different situation than an adult who develops an agnosia later in life. The great difference between adult agnosia and infantile agnosia is that the child never had the awareness for example of the size and shape of things. The loss of the memory of familiar objects, is then a different experience then to never know. This difference is a gulf between mother and child that is impossible to measure.

Many of the symptom problems of autism are the result of agnosias. Agnosia explains the empty stare these children often have when people enter their presence whether close family or total stranger. It also accounts for their total lack of interest in their surroundings, that must be a mass of shapeless nothings they cannot identify. Visual agnosia has been described as total or partial loss of the ability to recognize formations, objects by sight, or persons through sensory stimuli as a result of organic brain damage.

The brain has been mapped out to locate the relationship between injuries to the brain and signs and symptoms that result. Some findings are specific but there is overlap. Normal visual perception provides determination and discrimination of spatial [space] information, for example, position in space and relative objective size and location. Visual perception is not directly related to visual acuity or eye movements. In the autistic individual, memory previously stored in association cortices and related to objects' tactile or visual characteristics is impaired or lost. Affected persons sometimes can perceive the general nature of an object but not specific object. An example is prosopagnosia, the inability to identify well known faces, including close friends, despite being able to identify generic facial features. This must create frustrating experiences in an infant because of their lack of previous exposure.

A hands on form of visual-spatial agnosia is a syndrome consisting of failure to analyze spatial relationships and inability to perform simple constructional tasks under visual control. This syndrome is usually associated with lesions in the posterior portions of the occipital-parietal lobe of the right cerebral hemisphere in right handed patients. This is occipital lobe area that is the landing area for large bursts of intense light.

The affected individual often has an obsessive insistence of sameness and corresponding resistance to new things. This marked inflexibility may be strongly defended by 'temper tantrums' or rage attacks. It is clear the autistic child is able to enter into a rage, but to what is it aimed.

Color agnosia is a form of visual impairment verging on blindness. It is an inability to identify specific colors by sight caused by lesions of the occipital and temporal lobes. Again it is the landing site of bursts of high intensity light from the environment.

This agnosia is just part of the many problems autistic children have with shapes and forms. For example, it takes color sometimes to delineate trees in a forest otherwise they are simply a mass of strange shapes. Lack of color understanding is part of isolation. If color is limited to black and white, massive shapes such as trees or buildings can appear to be threatening. At a distance, this same problem could present itself when an autistic child is faced with a new group of people.

Localization agnosia is an inability to recognize the area where the skin is touched. Tactile agnosia is an inability to recognize objects by touch in the presence of intact cutaneous and preconception and sensation, caused by a lesion in the contralateral parietal lobe. Close to the visual lobe and at the same time having to do with the identification of areas of touch and objects to be seen, it is also an area of exposure to any bursts of intense bright light.

Another form of localization is called visual-spatial agnosia, which is more complex. It is an inability to recognize, or localize objects by sight, or to appreciate distance, motion and spatial relationships: usually caused by a lesion in that same bilateral parieto-occipital region. An object is anything to which thought or action is directed.

Tactile stimulus is very important in mothering. An early sign of autism is the baby's indifference to those who give care; They resist cuddling and do not display the usual anticipatory responses and postures for being picked up. They do not respond to maternal stimuli: for example when cradled they do not cuddle or adapt their self to the other individual. These symptoms are related to touch. This explains the autistic child's inability to mold their body to their mother or caregiver when picked to be carried, or held in her arms.

The parietal lobe is the portion of the cerebral hemisphere which extends from the central sulcus to the parieto-occipital fissure and near the level of the Sylvian Fissure. This area receives projections from the somato-sensory areas 5 and 7. Somato-sensory is sensation relating to the body's superficial and deep parts as contrasted to to specialized senses such as sight. Experimental studies indicate the body surface is projected dermatone by dermatone on the post-central gyrus.

Close to the visual lobe and at the same time having to do with the identification of areas of touch and objects to be seen, the somato-sensory areas 5 and 7, are also the area of exposure to any bursts of intense bright light. The most common agnosias are asterocognosis, [tactile agnosia] loss of the power to perceive the shape and nature of an object and inability to identify it by superficial contact alone. An object is anything to which thought or action is directed.

The hand is the human part that can touch the world around us. In the case of the hand that has "lost"; the skills of the hand or have been greatly reduced.

The area of the cortex seems to be necessary for interpretation for somatic sensory experiences.

Finger agnosia is an inability to name or recognize individual fingers of one's own or of other persons; most often caused by lesions of or near the angular gyrus of the dominant hemisphere.

Visual-spatial agnosia is an inability to localize objects or to appreciate distance, motion, and spatial relationships; caused by a lesion in the occipital lobe. The brain tissue involved here is just anterior to the visual cortex and part of the occipital-temporal-parietal union.

Tactile agnosia an inability to recognize objects by touch, in the presence of intact cutaneous and proprioceptive hand sensation; caused by a lesion in the contralateral parietal lobe.

Auditory agnosia is an inability to recognize sounds, words or music; caused by a lesion of the auditory cortex of the temporal lobe. This area has fibers connected to the visual cortex and is quite close to the visual cortex in location. It is part of the "union" of the occipital-temporal-parietal group that is so important in cognition. Hearing and speech are joined in the area of the temporal lobe which is just inside of the ears, and speech difficulty is a consistent problem in autistic children. Those symptoms are associated with disorders located in the temporal lobe. The auditory centers are very close to the visual centers and all are insulated by the thickest and hardest bone in the body. Because of that bony insulation it would be an area hard put to dissipate heat. Auditory characteristics includes, abnormal relationships, language disorders with impaired understanding, echolalia, and pronominal reversal particularly using "you" instead of "I" or me when referring to one's self; rituals and compulsive phenomenon [an insistence on the preservation of sameness], and uneven intellectual development with mental retardation in most cases. The auditory impairment and fear of loud noises are related to the hearing and balance neurological centers of the acoustic and balance systems by the ear and close to the visual lobes.

Another problem for the autistic child is their isolation which is compounded by their difficulties with speech and language. Damage by a large burst of bright light explains the strange sounds the autistic child makes such as echolalia. Echolalia is a parrot-like repetition of a word or a sentence just spoken to another person. The sounds they make are repeated countless times and there is no stopping them. Much of this comes from pathological changes temporal lobes. It is also seen with schizophrenia.

And then there is the oddity of walking in autistic children. In autistic children there is a strange caveat to walking. They may have little or no interest in learning to eat, use the toilet, or speak, though there is no difficulty in learning to walk. Like problems of late onset in autistic children, "The onset of walking and especially speaking is delayed." The reason for this is that the neuron center in the brain for walking is about as far from a light flash attack as any tissue in the brain. It is on top of the brain and anatomically centered there both horizontally and vertically.

There is another factor that is similar. In the brain, the tissue in the precentral gyrus has the role of governing basic movements. The tissue just anterior to the postcentral gyrus has the same specific role in relation to skilled movements. Both of these areas are near the crown or superior surface of the brain. This would make them relatively safe and out of harms way in case of a large burst of intense light by geographical location. Of all brain tissue this area would seem to be the most remote from a blast of intense light. The result is that walking can be delayed but not
destroyed.

Damage to visual area has confusing results. Both forms of visual agnosia create a gap between the autistic individual and those around him. While this is not blindness in its commonly understood form, the agnosia acts to leave an autistic child unable to make sense of the real world. The parts of masses seen by an autistic child might seem to be moving or loom larger while remaining motionless could only add to their lack of understanding and loneness. It is their world, a place they will defend. It is not so much that they march to a different drummer as it is that they just march.

19 THE CALCARINE CORTEX

There is an area that lies mainly in the calcarine fissure, located bilaterally on the medial aspect of each occipital cortex. Over the years it has become known as the calcarine cortex and by other different names suggestive of the area having almost global importance. They were the general interpretative area, the gnostic area, the knowing area, and so forth. A breakdown of the calcarine cortex is a central failure in the autistic brain. It is not just intellect and understanding that the child is missing. Damage to the calcarine cortex will create more than one agnosia at the same time. The more anterior parts of the calcarine area are concerned with peripheral vision. A human loses both object vision and light perception when the calcarine cortex is removed.

The occipital lobe or posterior lobe of the cerebral hemisphere is pyramidal in shape. The posterior occipital poles are mainly concerned with macular [central] vision. Known as the calcarine cortex [area 17] projects to area 18 [paristriate lobule], which in turn projects to area 19, [preoccipital area]. Visual function is localized in the occipital lobe, primarily in the calcarine cortex; [area striate, area 17 of Brodman.]. Areas 18 and 19 are visual association areas; lesions there cause disturbances in spatial orientation and visual word blindness [alexia]. Alexia, also known as optical blindness, an inability to comprehend the meaning of written or printed words and sentences. Word blindness serves to obviate the autistic child's dilemma. Basically for the child, even though their optics are normal their view is a scrambled field of odd shapes in strange colors or no colors at all.

It is a visual agnosia form of blindness there is basically a loss of visual appreciation of objects which are seen but not identified, even though visual acuity is normal. The cause is a lesion in area 18 of the occipital cortex. Area 19 receives projections from all parts of the cortex and then coordinates visual with other reflexes. It is then a fact that even though the individual with autism may have functioning eyes; it does not mean he or she can see and recognize the world around them in the same way as most of the human population.

Damage to the temporal lobes [the area of the temple] below and behind the primary auditory area often causes a person to lose his understanding of words or other auditory experiences even though he hears them. This is confounded by odd sounds, strange smells and tastes. It is probably the lack of touch that works against the mother-child relationship most. To cuddle is to transfer warmth, love, and protection; gifts no one else can give.

All of the interpretive areas meet one another in the posterior part of the [auditory] temporal lobe in the anterior part of the angular gyrus where the temporal, parietal and occipital lobes all come together. The area of confluence of the different sensitivities is especially highly developed in the dominant side of the brain and it plays the single greatest role of any part of the cerebral cortex in the higher levels of brain functions that are called "cerebration." Therefore this region has frequently been called by different names suggestive of the area having almost global importance: the general interpretive area, the gnostic area, the knowing area, and so forth. The temporal portion of the general interpretive area is also called Wernicke's area.

The ability of the visual system to detect spatial organization of the visual scene, that is, to detect the forms of objects, brightness, of the individual parts of the objects, shading, and so forth, is dependent on the function of the primary visual cortex. This area lies mainly in the calcarine fissure, located bilaterally on the medial aspect of each occipital cortex.

The macula is represented at the occipital pole of the visual cortex and the peripheral regions of the retina are represented in concentric arcs farther forward from the occipital pole. The pole is one of two points at the extremities of the axis of any organ. Thus, the pattern of contrasts in the visual scene is impressed upon the neurons of the visual cortex, and this pattern has a spatial orientation roughly the same as that of the retinal image. That places it in the middle of harms way for any mass of high intensity light with all of its photons, no matter its size. By bringing together most of the spatial senses to this interconnected crossroad; damage to the connecting fibers can act as a total or partial block to the messages traveling on the neural pathway.

Even though the calcarine cortex and its many attachments are in the far posterior of the brain, they are still quite vulnerable to strikes by bursts of intense light. That area with its many interconnections that claim much control in three lobes of the brain, and is connected with the rest, sits at the end of the optic nerves. This location is central to all light entering the brain. It is this area that is first met by any bolus or large bolt of intense light as it comes from the optic nerve and it is the same area where the light pauses, reverses direction and goes to the frontal lobe of the brain.

The calcarine cortex is directly connected to the site where light from the eyes pauses and then rebounds or spins around into reverse direction so that electro-physiologic messages are spread to the forebrain. Anatomically that portion of the cortex is next in line after the optic nerves and is the landing spot for messages transfer from the retina. The light is expected to come to a stop and do a 180 degree turn, an action which in the doing, will leave some of its heat, energy, and movement. After that, the turn around completed, and the remaining heat, energy and movement aboard, the remaining light streams off in the opposite direction to spread all over the brain and especially the frontal lobe.

That turn-about in the occipital lobe involves a momentary stop or hesitation for a period in brain tissue. Such a maneuver would certainly leave, unload, dissipate, or deposit, heat on the spot. The heat collected there would be a great portion of the amount of heat that entered the optic nerve plus body heat.

Their the loss of visual function, agnosia, is identical to the disconnect autistic children suffer when they stare out of their private world at us. One the most consistent and difficult problems for the autistic child is their inability to make sense of their surroundings. It lends to their need for sameness. Any change in their visual field can be frightful. Agnosias account for the autistic child's total lack of interest in their surroundings, that must be a mass of shapeless nothings they cannot identify. They are isolated from their environment and are more likely to relate to objects than people. That symptom group is a major portion of the cause of their loneness and their inability to connect with the world around them. For the infant the inability to take on the parenting which is offered in love and care, the connect that makes a child human and part of society is lost.

20 SLIGHT BUT GENERALIZED BRAIN DAMAGE

There is a great difference between an injury to a newborn's brain and that of an adult. An adult's brain is the finished product of human development. Usually an insult to the adult brain is met with a sturdy, and functioning organism that has a backup systems called a memory bank.

For the newborn it is quite the opposite, any change in their developing brain is magnified by altered or damaged architecture. Autism is a very slight but telling failure in the developmental change of infancy. In autism light and its direct effects are limited to the brain and parts of the spinal cord and it is in those areas that the disease is created. The postnatal period, the portion of development after birth, can extend for ten years and longer. Those formative years find the cell membranes made of delicate, thin, soft, film like tissue, that are easily injured. The newborn has a fragile batch of germinating cells that are vulnerable to stunting change, or total destruction. Because of the fragile and miniature make up of the baby it would not take much added temperature to damage the brain thereby crippling the normal development of its architecture and functional qualities.

It is not necessary to account for inordinate or large and constant repeated amounts of light. The amount of light received, whether child or adult, would be the same simply because of the camera and its schematics. In any case it is logical that the dose of damaging light in an infant would not need to be equal to an adult to cause harm because of the fragile make up of the infant brain. For the newborn just a few large bursts of high intensity light might cause a lot of trouble.

Then to, it may be easier to slip a burst of intense bright light into a newborn's brain because of the ineffectiveness of their blink response. The two month lag period of development of a proper blink response after birth, leaves the newborn completely vulnerable through a period in which many photos are made on babies. Under certain circumstances, light with all of its heat, energy, and movement, can reach the greater part of the brain where it is difficult to escape. The brain rests in a closed compartment, the skull, with a resting temperature of 98.6 F.

In autism a powerful wave of light is able to engulf the nerve pathways sweeping through and flooding the parts of the brain starting with the calcarine cortex, and parts of the temporal lobes. The landing field of the light in the calcarine cortex would take the greatest punishment from heat created by the light. This bright light penetrates the brain changing from light [photons] to electro-magnetic signals. Heat, energy, and movement travel into the visual lobes reverse direction and spread into the forebrain, and leaving a deposit or load of heat in the calcarine cortex. In the calcarine cortex the heat of the overload of light, with no way to displace its light factors, would burn, melt or boil local tissue while sending the rest of the light along toward the frontal lobes.

The direct effects of too much light seem to be limited to the eye until there is severe overload but there is the fact of the difference between newborns and adults. In either case, a large load of light and the heat created by it travels through the optic nerve and into a limited area of the brain. At that point, permanent damage is limited to children.

Some of the lower parts of the brain and much of the spinal cord are not exposed to the direct light and thus spared of damage. As to the relationship of the first sign or symptom of autism in relation to the date of childbirth; everyone seems to agree that the disease starts early, quite early. For many who deal with autism the disorder seems to be caused by some sort of an environmental agent. Why it would be more common in little boys than in little girls is not clear. It may be that boys develop their light reflex later than girls. Generally boys mature slower than girls.

21 THE HYPOTHESIS COMONALITIES & CONSISTENCY

The hypothesis is consistent with damage to bran of a newborn. The tissue of a newborn is not just maintaining itself; it is growing and forming changes that will continue for years after birth. This vulnerable period is marked by changes in size and architectural change as well. Any death, damage or distortion of cells that occurs during that period of time can make lifelong changes to the baby.

The autistic child has an illness derived from a disorder of the brain. The illness does not seem to 'run in the family' or be genetic.

The ability to make and operate extremely bright lighting systems aimed at newborns and very young children during photography has the potential to thrust large bursts of high intensity light into the eyes of the vulnerable.

The first appearance of autism and the introduction of photography are not exactly in lock-step but, Kanner's description of the disorder and the use of augmentation lighting are closely related. Just the recognition of autism took some time. A second cause of lag time was the problem of differentiating autism from childhood schizophrenia. That time period would have been the difference between the first flash of light synchronized with photographic exposure and the earliest known cases of autism.

Invasions of the brain by large bursts of light are consistent with the supposition that autism is the result of an environmental agent.

There is also the appearance of what is now called background lighting. That light, which seems to be everyplace, adds baseline heat, energy and movement to any amount delivered by a flash bulb. Many people use flash attachments in daylight.

As early as the time of their birth, babies are photographed. From that time on infants are photographed routinely with standard cameras augmented by extremely bright lights often referred to as “flash guns” or “flash bulbs.” New and more complex equipment can now run in serial order as “motion picture” film and television with continuous bright lights.

The hypothesis is consistent with autism being a disease that appears very early in life. It is that characteristic that separates it from childhood schizophrenia.

The hypothesis supports and is consistent with the fact that large bursts of intense light, heat, energy, and movement can destroy brain tissue. Destruction of the calcarine cortex and other parts of the brain can create symptoms of autism. The problem the autistic child has with recognizing objects includes people.

By building a disconnect to people, the child is alone with only his fantasy to drive the content of thought. In classical instances of autistic thinking such as occurs in schizophrenia the unconscious sphere makes largest contribution to autism. It is a sort of thinking that is limited by hallucination and imagination.

This hypothesis is consistent with the fact that autism could be the product of a slight or minimal burn of brain tissue that is spread out through the brain.

This is also consistent with the idea that burn damage can follow the track of neural pathways of the brain. It is then consistent with the fact that once heat gets into the brain any burn will take advantage of the fact that some brain tissue has no [wrap around its neurons] insulation and many of the neuron pathways of the brain are covered by a mylin-sheath which is the insulation made of fatty substances that are combustible.

It is consistent with heat delivered to brain cells that then become swollen and broken leaving neural pathways blocked permanently. It is as if the dendrites rather than the whole of the neuron is injured.

The hypothesis is consistent with known destructive effects of light on the human visual system. This includes permanent blindness from too much light, Retinitis pigmentosa, and Macula lutea, and the light of an atomic bomb. All of these injuries are caused by light. But there is a difference. The damage that appears in autism is inside the brain and across the optic nerves from the eye and eye-socket which are outside of the bony cranium. The optic nerves are fairly large and sturdy compared to the neural pathways of the brain. Hence, the hypothesis is consistent with the location of a big hit of light and its effects, in area 19. This would also include changes in loci areas 17, and 18. It is also consistent with the many problems that develop with the calcarine cortex and its connections which are many and varied.

Large bursts of light gaining entrance to the brain is also consistent with the cornea, the lens, and the eye in general, as very powerful gatherers of light directed straight to the eye and ultimately to the brain.

The hypothesis explains that damage due to large bursts of light that can cause different injuries in children than they do in adults. Thus the result autism, is not so much different due to different doses of light but rather due to age and development of the individual.

The hypothesis is consistent with all of the problems of agnosia that interfere with or cripple the individual's ability to live in, join into or take part in the world of reality. In this way the hypothesis is consistent with the chief symptoms of autism and explains much of their behavior.

It is consistent in its involvement with the stereographical vision system which is spread out in the brain in about the same layout as vision. Also, the hypothesis is consistent with word blindness.

With this hypothesis timing is crucial. It is consistent with an infant's lack of a blink response until as late as two months of age. In the circumstance of serial bursts of intense light, the hypothesis is consistent with damage being created in a infant because the reflex can become exhausted. The characteristic of the lid blink responding to foreign bodies or jolts of bright light might be to slow to protect the eye in any case, but if that is so it leaves the child vulnerable to bright light during a period in which many photographs are made.

Many photographs are portraits made of people at special events and pictures of newborn are practically a ritual. The first and most vulnerable period is after delivery and the period just after which produce many photos. Birthdays and birthday parties seem to demand recording by pictures but mankind seems to think many reasons to take pictures of kids.